THEE ALCHEMIST'S MAGIC DRAGON THEATER

A Manuscript Of Original Esoteric Poetry

By

Jerry Louis

Thee Alchemist's
Magic Dragon Theater

Edited by Linda Louis

Dedicated to my wife Linda and my lovely daughters Daria, Alethea, and Artemis. My granddaughters Ashley, Sierra, Annabella, and my great granddaughter Delilah

ISBN 978-1-105-47131-5

FORWARD

ABOUT THE AUTHOR AND THE ESOTERIC POETRY

Jerry Louis, Co-Founder and Co-Director of the Archimedes Foundation, which was formed as a Foundation for the advancement of the Creativity of the "Human Soul", was a Clinical Hypnotist and Past Life Age Regressionist for over 10 years.

I have dedicated my Poetry to the psychological transformation of the "ALCHEMY OF THE SOUL" to a higher expression, contact of itself, and the incorporation of past life talents and abilities so the individual may use them to benefit and enrich their life in this present incarnation. The Akashic Records are a memory tape recording; so to speak, of every one of our Soul's experiences. These past life recordings are contained and located within each of our physical brains, there to be retrieved and consciously contacted through the help of a Hypnotist and Past Life Age Regressionist that understands the "Human Path Of The Soul".

The social implications of the incorporation of Reincarnation into modern society would mean that each and every Soul would have access to unlimited creative, artistic, intellectual genius and human potentials learned before in previous lives and the ability to incorporate these creative "Past Life Abilities" and use them in their present incarnation to enrich their life in the now.

It would be truthful to say that each individual should not follow Masters, just their teachings are important. Every person should follow "No One" but the "Path Of Their Own Soul" and this can be manifested through the use of creative endeavors; such as: Artists, Writers, Poets, Actors, Musicians, Dancers and many other art forms creating individual Soul contact. The main message being conveyed is to follow your own Soul's path and no one else's. To be kind, loving and compassionate to all living beings and to make an effort to try in some way to make this world a better place for all of mankind to live together in Peace, Happiness and Harmony!

THEE ALCHEMIST'S MAGIC DRAGON THEATER suggests what is the nature of the Soul, contact and a higher expression of the Human Soul. This Esoteric Poetry Book is veiled and entrenched in symbolism, Spiritual affirmations, Metaphysical knowledge, Esoteric Philosophy and Hypnotically induced trance Poetry. Since matters of the Soul such as

Reincarnation or Religious matters have never been proven to exist by Science, they must be looked at as Legend, Fantasy and Mythology and therefore these Poems must not be taken literally but looked at Symbolically.

Being a Bohemian, Pacifist, Naturalist and Esoteric Philosopher, I also attempt to fuse with the Human Soul, The Akashic Records, Past Life Age Regression, Alchemy and Reincarnation with our Mother Earth and our Cosmic Universe. I hope that you have lots of fun tripping through time and space, trancing out and conjuring up the Allegories.

This Esoteric Poetry Book is 100 of my best Poems selected from 500 lifetime Poems spanning over 40 years.

TABLE OF CONTENTS

THEE ALCHEMIST'S MAGIC DRAGON THEATER

Welcome to Thee Alchemist's Magic Dragon
Theater
The light show is about to begin
An assortment of precious Colored Gems and
Crystal Balls are aligned upon a magic wheel
Spinning with glowing candle power rotating in
The center with winged Gem Amulets on the
Outer edge with colors glowing and spinning out
Of the Crystal Balls releasing the Devic
Elementals
Creating a kaleidoscope of a psychedelic light
Show in a dark room flashing everywhere which
Is most pleasing to the eyes and spirit
A light show of true delight is awaiting for your
pleasure
Come one, come all to Thee Alchemist's Magic
Dragon Theater.

THE ALCHEMIST'S CHAMBER

Down to the secret room
Lay the Alchemist's Chamber.

Surrounded with base minerals and gems
everywhere
A fire hearth with crucible, mortar, pedestal and
Table with his own Soul's life book
Of his Akashic Records containing his Souls Past
Life's journeys
Through endless time
Lay there on the table with hourglass, amulets,
Crystal balls, candles and crystal skull with quill
and ink.

This was the Alchemist's study table where
He prepared before performing
The Ancient Art of Alchemy

An eight pointed star was painted
On the chamber floor with a rotating throne
In the middle of the star

There he performed his Nature Magic
And the ancient Art of Alchemy making
Gold and precious gems using the
Electromagnetic field of our earth's gravity, the
Devic Elementals and time creating Thee
Alchemist's Magic Dragon Theater.

THE RETURN OF THEE ALCHEMIST

The Return of Thee Alchemist
The sparked schism
The flowering apple tree
The pale appetite
The inscribed attitudes
The Sacred Sword's

That maker of Gold
That Healer of old
That imparted Hearted
That degrading up-grader
That harp-head happy
Of the tricks of spun heads
To witch the game is undead.
Floating endlessly about my trough
The innocent gain of think
Are Souls engraved in ink?

A FLASH OF MYSTIC DHARMA

A Flash Of Mystic Dharma
Upon that Cosmic Plane of infinity
Bestowed of many grips
Of hands that were upheld
Shield arms for Humanity.

The sword of thrashing tongue
The pen of gashing ink
Dock birthed, but not enthroned
Instructed, but not forlorned
The in-creeping hand of torn.

CONJURE UP THE ALLEGORIES

Secret Dreams for holding on
Solves what you can't have
When you are awake.
Liquid visions of night's necessities
True to inkwell for your sake
Speeds the arrow to your fate.

If you listen and approximate
You might Conjure Up The Allegories
In your paradoxical lifetime.
Thus soothing and exhaling for your
Cosmic Mind
An Art, very true to find
Of what is looking at your Third Eye
An easy way to trace.

OH LITTLE POETS

Oh Little Poets that you are
Please come along your way.
The dreams of yesteryear
Unlocked in today's scenes
Please bring yourself, your way.

You learned to write
Just like yesterday and before
Please remind yourself, that you can
So you may write, what you learned before
And bring it to this day.

The knowledge locked inside of children
Must be helped, to release.
They knew so much when they were big
Now they have little feet.
Please bring that memory back to them.
Please remind them
That they're adults in children's bodies
And that they know more than they think

Please bring me Emily Dickinson and
Edgar Allen Poe
I know they're walking around.
Please help them realize
Just how important they are
To release their wisdom somehow

The days will unwind and time will remind them
Of the special gifts that they are
To release with me their secret dreams
And help Humanity's Strife.

THE UNPOLISHED CHALICE

Sold out on a trick
Of the most demise
Torn of what Rim?
The Unpolished Chalice

Scorpionic happenings
Think that I have been.
Cups unfold of blood wine spilled
Vats participate in oft thrill.
To reap the drink of Life not led.
For as long as there's a Sip
The necessary experience needed is on display.

ALCHEMICAL CIRCUMSTANCE

Alchemical Circumstance
Made by Liquid Chance
All is true to what has been performed.
Sacrificial Altar of sweet remorse
Destined from the first day of conversion
To be wronged by the time death of a truth.

Because sweet as it is
Is now and forever short lived
Time spent finding out what has happened
Is time lost of the true reality

But life has built up a wall
No matter how thin, tender, and small
Waylaid for sometime
Harked and reclined.

THEE ALCHEMIST SPOKE

To each his own
Thee Alchemist Spoke
The dreams were never untold.
Secret seal of un-bred deals
You make with the golden Sun.

Torn by what ideal thought?
Spoken by what unsealed mouth?
The eye of reflect, introspect
The gills of fish not caught.
Entrenched sand of loosened feet
The land is liquid and we are heat.

PIECES OF LEGEND

Pieces Of Legend
Unspoken sentence
Of life's realities
I know that you're pleased.
The Scepter unleashed
Of the truth revealed
Why do we have
Hands that feel?

Why do we in the course of life led
Do we see the Love action fully displayed
Of the multi return of our Soul's
Why do we come and go?
Why do we Yin and Yang?

I think that explains
Why we can, why we must
Sorcery action always forward moving
Crashing the firefall like once and before
What falls to the ground rises up again.

SOUL INDESTRUCTIBLE

For I am the Paradox of Life
For I am not here
For I am, really here
For I am, not Born
For I am, Reborn
For I am, Dead
For I am, not Dead

For I am, in this place where expression
Has its way Ethericly
For I am, the Elixir of Life
For I am, The Soul Indestructible
For even though, I am dead
For I am, always Alive.
For I have come, to this Earth
For I have gone, from this Earth
For I will always be here and there
For I am infinitely Immortal
For I am the Philosopher's Stone
For I am at other places at the same time
For I am not Born
For I am not Dead
For the Dead have arisen
For I am not Dead.

TO DASH THE STARS

The Raven caws in peace delight.
But the shadow never ends at night.
The heralding time for which he caws
Of time unspoken, of time unbent.
Leaves me with all that is not dreamt
In the naked night of dawn

Peaceful, but strong bird of flight
Your claws of strength are rare bird.
But strange rare bird of vision
All you want left is to freedom fly.
All you want left is To Dash The Stars.

MAGIC CHANT

Peace in time, Spirit rhymes
The spoken words, of Sacred Mother Nature
Magic Chant, you can absorb through your skin
Wishing spells and clichés, left to you after birth.
The earth wants you, so leave today
Humanity wants you, so I'm on my way.

Lead yourself to the troupe, the Sacred Group
Go to the place you want to, now you're there
Left in its place, was only one.
Your hereditary genes, of what you know
Is at your fingertips.
Breathe out all ignorance and hate
Breathe in the oxygen of our life
Suck in the benevolent power of the free
corpuscles.

YOUR AKASHIC RECORDS

Ready to see Your Akashic Records
Ready to see you're Past Lives' Scripts
Ready to see your Soul's path record
Ready to see your Soul's Archetypes of days gone by?

Time not kept in bliss, said the Alchemist
Signed for sorted Souls
Pleaded for silly gain
Not that what may remain
Sold for a coin at one time
Never regained, the real time line.

Only force yourself to serve your Soul.
Be your Soul's procurer
Be your Soul's intruder
Be your Soul's vicar
Be your Soul's desire.

UNFIXED IN TIME AND SPACE

Unfixed In Time And Space
Time traveling on blazing sidesaddle
Elite and traversed
Explicit in structures
Foundations enthroned
The Alchemist was symbolically entombed
Wrapped and amused
Of the front fourth Dimension, that was backlogged forever
Imps of information were short changed and with held
For the latter parts, of forthwith.

TRICKS THE CLOWN

By the taste of his hands
On a sunny sand dune day
Of points of disguise in anyone's eyes
Of healing green scenes masked and arranged

Twirling spiral sights fall down
Unfixed before my mind and down
Tricks The Clown not spoken seen
Forces him into in between
The karmic balance, place unseen

Inspect your clock time heart
Make sure you are that part not seen
Which searches each day for the Mystic
Knowledge
Of Truth, the Dual, of Life not led.

YOUR ARCHETYPAL PROTOTYPE

In long life's distant dreams
The Alchemist's Heart is saved
With many distorted schemes and hidden rhymes
At my door, street, and way.

To clock the Life of mysteries down
Give to your Archetypal Prototype.
Love, Take, and Facilitate
Do all he tells you to do.

On the Path of Initiation the Adept decides to Incarnate The Archetypal Prototype which is a Divine Possession of a previous life now a Cosmic Solar Angel which wishes to reincarnate Into his present future life in the now, to have Once and again, a cosmic being in the physical Form to perform White Magic, Healing and Alchemy once and again on this physical Plane of existence.

TUNE OF THE SOUL UNLEASHED

And they told him what not to inscribe
And he listened to them, and inscribed
not the truth
And draweth he did of the Heart not displayed
And sung not the Tune Of The Soul Unleashed
And hung on the sound of the head not spoken.

For to reach the dark, you can embark
On a journey that shows no light.
For if you show the light to a darkened society
You will only blind them
And drive them deeper into their darkest pit.

Secret!
Keep the light veiled both night and day.
Silent secret your wishes and arrows
That someone may lift the hidden veil
Thus revealing them selves!

THE ABYSS OF INFINITY

Interesting motions of thoughts not formed
Leaves me with the Threshold Of Id.
Un-fluxed tension of Heart remorse
Shows you the strength of bent forlorned.
Of Heart not bent I say to thee
Give me of Heart felled Soul.

Of eye hole, of passage, of no return
Immortality crashes right through you.
Of the vortex of the not reached sheath
Give my Soul the strength to handle the grasp
Of the tearing of the fabric of my spiritual thread.

Upon reaching The Abyss Of Infinity
Give me the intuition to unwind my task.
Exploding mind of invocative dreams
Give me the Spirit to see through scenes
To unwind the past, of thoughts not said
To hold all forms, happy in thine head.

OF DRINK OR BE SPILLED

Of pleasing past
Of truth not told
Of sealed Souls
Of Heart's that were once
Of those that know
Of life not leading.
Of stories unfold
Of silent secret harmony
Of love, joy, and in between
Of minds thoughts that can't be seen
Of the death of life's honesty
Of the vows of hope's fidelity
Of overcoming life's tricks of anarchy
Of sacred disease
Of computerized illness
Of much to fulfill
Of Drink Or Be Spilled.

THE VOID OF CONCEPTION

The strange will scare you
The freaks, you can fear
Their ideas are new
And alive like flesh.
Asking each minute to conquer the world
But mostly falling into a trance
They will flash right through your vibes
Only to leave you to be Hypnotized
In dread of what you don't know why

Lost there in despair
No where to go except
The freedom from negative weight thought.
Staring into your eyes
With a flash of light
You fall into The Void Of Conception.
The truth of your inner Soul lies within
To burn,
To clean,
To intervene.

THE GOLD OF WHAT I HAVE FOUND

Intrepid speech
My mouth employs
Is touchy sure indeed.
I wish my mouth
To set and play
On death and honesty.

To wash the stones
Of life's rocks will
And hold it in my hands
And give to other people
The Gold Of What I Have Found.

May the sad turn happy
May the weak grow strong
May the abandoned find warmth
May the scorned find strength within
May the withdrawn find happiness without.

OF OLDEN TIMES TRUE

Of night betwixt
In dark lonely sleeps bliss
I think I will travel tonight.
Of nights dream train
I know the tract
Of which way, we all have been.

Of blue dream streams which
Flows into sacred rivers
Think I will gravitate this night
To the Loved Ones of time, past and future
Of friends of new, that we knew in times olden.
Of friends of old, that are of olden days stand
still.
Of the faith, of the future
Of Olden Times True
I'd like to find the best of you.

SEVERAL FATHOMS

Several Fathoms
On countless occasions
A number of repentances
Were already being made.
Efforts were thrown by the wayside
Countless causes were spying in
The eyes stood out, in the night, looking in
Realizing the knowledge
In very move we make.
Speaking the unspoken
Saying the unsaid.
Reciting what as been recited to
For the sake of being
Is being for the sake?

INSIDE MY DREAMS

In richer times not born I see
Shaded scenes Inside My Dreams.
Strange Past Life Forms that haven't been
Reach for the physical, and try to come in.
Unspoken words of fate, I hear
Listen to the distance between your ears.
Unraveled traps of life, I see
Train gauge of life, I measure.
Dreams unlocked of other days
Torn of what I'm taught to see
That latter I may live these days.

THE NATIVES ARE WILD

Time the heart of sadness sorrow
Lift the mind to untimely reaches.
Cleanse the earth of evil magic
Use the heart to see the white light.
Gift not received from the Great One's
Unduly mind to rest or pant.
The not reached Soul you gasp for air
Trails of justice are lost by the wayside.

To sad your sorrow keeping thrust
Lost in the void of energy waste
Emit a radar thinking, much to my reward.

Search the sinking bile of disgust
You rot the inside creeping.
Oh un-bred world that you are
Your jungles are here
Your Natives Are Wild.

MAGIC SOUL GUIDE

The voice said
Listen to yourself.
Who said that?
Was the first reply.
The man knew not from whence it came.
The voice said, from within
It's your Heart on your Head
It's your higher self, crowning thine own Head
Calling on your inner purpose dwelt.

Please through Telepathy, listen to him
He is your seed thoughts
From your higher planes of existence
Allowing you, to allow yourself
To drop seeds into your own consciousness
Listen to you, he knows you well
Listen to your Heart, he likes you too

Next time when I am spoken to by myself
I will listen carefully, and take heed.
For he knows much
For he is you.
Magic Soul Guide
You can't hide
Come to the surface
I love the load.

LIKE GENTLE RAIN

Placement of Divine Will
The Critics said to join.
The only hour left
Was that but to destroy
The only hope that the Spirit spoke
Was that Witch, which lifts the Heart
I think they will invest themselves
In action very smart.

To play with Hearts
Of Wills unleashed
Is a touchy state indeed
Just Like Gentle Rain, you must explain
Why you must help, and why people need.
This is why your actions
Have been given over to your own inner Soul
To work and assist The Great Ones inside
To be driven like a horse in stride
And sweat at sweet works Sojourns.

THE GHOST IN BETWEEN

Placement in the hands of the giver
I thought that I would never
Seek Young Trees of thought undreamt
In the weary hour of my Soul's introspect.

Rising Young Tree's of secret wisdom
Your trunks are huge
Your branches space into the heavens
Your roots are as deep
As the hot liquid core within the earth

Wingless teachers of the future
Your work is much
Your Heart is endlessly abounding.
The world awaits your words entrusted
To save Peace, Harmony, and The Ghost In
Between.

SPLASH THE SEASONS

Makes
What gives you a chance to partake
Silly songs that Soul your break
Torrid Rap
Someone smacked you upside the head.
Saying, "You're not alive".
Live and breathe the Life what you cannot die.

Head in hole of home
Give to me what you cannot go
Throw the pieces into one
Splash The Seasons down to the ground.

OF A WISHING SPELL

The bewitchment of time
Of peace denied
Magic charms always end that way.
Space of the dreams, you do not mean
To tear the pages of yesteryear
The Forces of the Weak are in dire need
Of the tension released, will help come along
their way.

If you know Of A Wishing Spell
That can dispel this Emanation
Please partake today.
If you know of some Wings we can borrow
Please send them quick.
If you know of some Incantations we can use
Please Chant them fast.

THE MUSIC OF THE SPHERES

Oh un-bred Horses of cosmic time planes
Listen to your feet stomp to
The Music Of The Spheres.
Can your animal heart
Hear the calling of The Great Ones
Who know all, and tend our Sacred Mother
Nature?

Can you hear the resounding, pulsating
Beat of Life endearing?
Hope will find the magic of delight
Calling on Nature.

More than their animal desires
To Tear The Flesh Of Humanities Graves.

THE CLASP OF VICE

Talked into believing
My Soul went astray.
Laughed with the Dragon Himself
Until I figured out
That I had stocks invested in the Beast
Which was part of me
And part of everyone else

For it was the man
That had thought the hatred
That he had thought himself.

And the Dragon was in him
And the Dragon was about him.
Only to be held
By The Clasp Of Vice
Aching with glutton
You drew another day
Of investing in your own demise.

IN THE LAND OF PHARAOH

In The Land Of Pharaoh
Down by the Nile
Secrets hide within her waters
Deep in the murk of mud.

But the secrets in her waters
Is not kept just there.
For it floats, endlessly
In the sky, earth, and universe.

Only waiting to be tapped into though Telepathy
By the intangible use of the brainwave
Oh wave of light I call to thee
To give me strength to see so deep.

OF BALANCED THOUGHT WEIGHT

Inscribed what telepathic vision
Entailed what sacred intrusion
Impaled elements of joyfulness.
Impeccable tastes of syndrome
Impeaching manner of disdain.

Unearthed tracks of bent not kneeling
Unannounced distortion of works
Unmasked by the mass of the Holy Weak
Unveiled by the hand of the Alchemist.
Unraveling speak, unspoken has been said
Understanding the process Of Balanced
Thought Weight.

PILLAR OF FIRE

Fiction unfolds the life of tomorrow
Present holds the now.
Yesterday is gone and past
I wish to remember them somehow.

Past Lives that have led me
To where I am now
Is the sum total of all of my being
Becomes my strength, called now.

Pillar Of Fire
I must move on
My work is incomplete.
I need some time
To heal some wounds
A few more rhymes
Before my life is to be complete.

THE CREEPING OF SUCH USAGE

The impeccable taste of thirst
The dry Heart of knowledge
The moist drip of seepage
The flow of blood thirst knowledge
The neuro-knowledge of the Brain Wave
The infusion of the Cosmic Mind
The intangible use of the Brain Wave
The Creeping Of Such Usage
The influx of your Heart traipsing.

THE ONES TO LOVE

Silent secret harmony
Gifted and laid upon my back
Turns to focus on special days
You loved the ways of love, and then they said to stay.

Mailed happiness in a letter
Someone said, hope your doing better.
Presents, which we all do trade, saying
I thought the warmth, was here this year.

Thought not gift was the subject
And they stared right into my eyes.
Cherish what lift they were the gifts
They were The Ones To Love.

THE JACK OF DIAMONDS

Speaking of the thought
Everything was in line.
The King had dealt with the Ace
And the Queen had tried hard.
The Jack was running around
Trying to secure the Diamonds.

Trying to make everything
Come down and through
For the interested two
All in touch
It was me in the clutch
I was in the interested two.

THEE ALCHEMIST STOOD ALONE

Thee Alchemist Stood Alone
As the Sprit of Silence spoke to him
As the Death of Silence listened in
We all held our heads
To The Death of Truth
Of what, we heard
Of what, we know
Of what's been told
Of what, is real

Death was at the end of the street for our Mentor.
Protégé's broke down and cried
At the end of the Oration

We knew The Alchemist had betrayed Himself
on purpose.
Destined to swallow his own magical words
To the Death of Silence without recourse
Unless the karmic deed was unraveled
immediately
Death would be instantaneous forever.

THE SACRED CREED

I bend myself down to you
Hoping that you will see me through
Hoping that you will see me stay
Just for the love of every days.

Just for the love of every days
I will see you if I can.
I will touch inside the back of your brain
Just to show you that I care
About giving you a chance
In the Human Jungle

Where people stalk for what they want
And strain for what they may.
Grasping for that last bit of need
They will find it if they lived by
Their Sacred Creed.
The Sacred Creed
Of Invisible Circular Truth.

STUFF YOUR MOUTH WITH CANDY

I've tried and tried, lived and died
Mostly wished my Soul would fly.
Got my way when I really wanted
Threw away what I didn't think
Spoke my mind what it would drink
Tried to care for others of what wasn't mine
To be fair in thought of jealous waste

And when the Just talked to my brain
I taught the not just what they may
That what we are, is not absolutely always right
It is what is Truth for standing.

Oh Heart, you speak of what you want
As you Stuff Your Mouth With Candy.
You know not when to stop your obese flight
You think all you do is right.

A MAGIC POTION, I RECALLED

The incarnation of happiness
What a joy to see, what cosmic plane could it be
Un-bred act of happiness
Knows just what to be

Laugh at yourself, they did install
A Magic Potion, I Recalled
In-placed, entrusted, until duty delights
To mow the sadness down like flock
To cheer the sorrow bearing throne
Of a sudden death truth I cannot escape
I think I'll enjoy myself, while I wait.

Harp-Head happy
Of the situation that is entrusted
The Dharmic job is clear.
Inhabited by the conditions abounding me
I must fight my Sword through clear.
Until the Id Of Demand calls impatiently
I must not waste I must not wait
Crashing the walls I think is best
Caught in Esoteric Retrospect.

PAST LIFE'S REALITIES

When you can see, Past Life's Realities
You can see into the deep blue sea.
When you fly above the mountains
All by yourself
You can see what Life's cards have dealt.
When you give up, Just let yourself be.
You could doubt yourself
But you wouldn't feel free.

When the silver Foxes feet have flown
You know the Moon's work has done its deeds.
When you look at something all by yourself
You can find the reason, at any Telepathic depth.

RAINBOW EYE'S

A poet listens to himself
And paints with pen what he hears and sees
Listen to your ears
And watch your eyes
They are your friend and helper.
Listen to your Solar Angels
They are your guiding light.

A Poet listens, and hears his Heart resounding.
With his mind and heart as partners
He can't go wrong.
Silver Tongue, teach me to learn
Golden Throat, we are patient
Rainbow Eye's, I see and believe.

HUMAN TIME MACHINES

We are Human Time Machines.
At night we exit our dream threads
Outside the pineal gland
On the top of our crowning heads
And journey to many nights dreamscapes
While slumbering in midnights sleeps repose.

With the help of a Past Life Age Regressionist
We are able to be placed
Into the twilight state of consciousness
And while still fully conscious, we are able to
Time Travel
To Past Lives and review the endless Sojourning
Of our Souls through endless time with the help
Of a Hypnotist who knows the "Human Path Of
The Soul"
Indeed we are Human Time Machines.

SPIRIT THOUGHTS

I thought of you
As real as you are
As far away as the Northern Star.
Hoped, blessed, wished and guessed
Tried as many can't forget.
Silly, sacred, laughed and prayed
Easy tomorrow, easy yesterday
Many memories have been endeared
Lost and easy, give I fear
Of all the life's, long years
And hold it, in our Hearts
We all need a fair start
And spoken in my dreams
All knowing what they need.
For them the life of Soul to give
Spirit Thoughts, words not said.

HALLUCINATION

Bare and naked
In my minds midnight dawn
Meteors crashing into my body
Leaches wrenching at my study
Seaweed twisted, tangled my motion
Slowed down my motivation
And gave me an inclination
Someone better know
How to stop this Hallucination.

THE MASK OF WIT

Scratching at our pillows
On nights chase dreams event
We fell down a long abyss.
Once and again our Souls fate met
The Mask Of Wit.

Clawing at our faces
Like Heaven and Hell was on our heads.
Dream flying, time traveling
Night running and pursuing we went
Trying to live the life we have spent
Only to discover that we crossed too far
The Abyss where we die every night
The Abyss where we sleep every night
The Abyss out of our bodies every night.

SPIN THROUGH TIME AND SPACE

Spin through Time and Space
Was the Alchemist's cosmic game
But the story was always untold.
The eyes stood out
In the Cosmic Globe
But they never realized
That the hidden secrets would unfold.
Only to realize it later on
Another Life, Another Planet
What dimension was The Alchemist caught on
this time?

OFF IN WHAT SPACE?

The influx of syndrome
The sparkle of delight
The infectious appetite

All the silent, secret magical discussions
Upon, imperiling infusion
Tracks the Heart of vision
Into Heart felled Soul.
To time left, be told
Speak of you unfold
To time left, be past seen
To time left, speak unsaid
Listen to your Heart be bold
Please time plane, open and behold.
Say mind game, it's your move.
Say time track, off into transverse
Say what Ohm name, Off In What Space?

THE WILL OF THE ELDERS

Of broken pieces, not touched I see
Of shaded scenes inside my dreams.
The unlocked spaces, you sojourn there
To be instructed in truth debate
To listen and reply to your night teachers
Do you dare not listen to your Heart?
Do you dare not listen to the resounding voice of pulsating life?

For it throbs through you and in you
And it through you and you through it.
Purify thine own self
With your Heart crowning thine own head.
Make thine own head
The Will Of The Elders.
For we, The Will Of The Elders, are!

THEE INCANTATION

Oh throat of speech
My Heart calls unto thee
From on top of thine own Head.
Removing the sheath of the voice box
Causing a triple play of flowing

The Triangular River of Intuition, The Sparkle of
Crystal Prisms
The Vestures of Antique Fusion
You only said, Thee Incantation.

THE IMPARTED SEEDS

Oh secret Brothers and Sisters of time and space
not kept.
Give me the hope and encouragement
To hold my electromagnetic cross steady in the
light
To hold steadfast my shadow in the dark
To dance and fence with paper and ink
To reveal, The Imparted Seeds, that I need.

To help all Spiritual knowledge to be released
To neutralize all negative power plays in life
So that common people will not be oppressed.
To learn from sacred Mother Nature
The laws of our Planetary Cosmic Force
To share in harmony with everyone everything
that is bliss.

RUN THROUGH THE FIREFALL

Upon the many endless pages
Of the countless Sages
That I have lived through
The many Spirit Ages
Of times, inset recline.

Up mounts the marksman
Of the Sparked Achilles heels
Dashing the endless streets
Upon midnights random dream chase

To fill the high stand
Of the Love give willing
You are swelled with feelings
Of the hands, gripping the Universe.

Being torn and crashed
With much heart bred stealing
You Run Through The Firefall
But you really had no chase.

THE MOON PATH OUT

The imperiled wishes of mankind
The Spirits left their vehicles
After a polarizing stay on this third dimension.
Before they leave this planetary sphere
These Spirits must wait for the time certain.
As they come in as Devic Group's
The path out, the same is also
A triple planet play of creation takes place.

The zenith of the Sun has many functions.
One of its functions is to keep a constant eye on the Moon
But for a short precious period of time
The Moon tricks the Sun
And hides itself behind the earth.
The darkness comes
The Devic Group's path is open
The Spirits exit the blackened Moon
The awaiting Spirits exit the bowels of the Earth.

Only to open up to other Devic Spirits awaiting
The Sun Path In
As once and before, and again and again
World with end
The Moon Dark Path Out
The Dark Full Moon.

THE SUN PATH IN

The appealing dreams of scenes
The uproaring scheme of plans
The torch of the seekers hand

The path of the sacred Sun
Is the path of the zenith of the Sun
The path of the secret Moon
Entrenched before the forward Sun
Magnifies an energy focal point of light.
A triple planet, line up play
A magical magnetic takes place

In from the spheres of the cosmic Universe
In flowing Angels of light and daring
Spirits of light, we all flow in
Groups of Spirits fly in as groups
For as groups, they lived the never ending
Play of creation in yesteryear life before

Groups of ancient nations
Come back, as once and before
To karmicly work out the play of creation
As once and before, and again and again called
The Oversoul
World without end
The Sun Light Path In
The Dark Full Sun.

THE ID OF DEMAND

Of Ancient Magic Theory
The mind wanted to time travel
So asking is receiving.
So the Alchemist's mind had time traveled there
And duty of delight, the glowing burden
The blazing fixed Eye did entrust.

Of peering fields of the Sorcerers scope
Of masked Angels of Light
The miss crept mouth gasps for air.
To bring vestures of an invisible Butterfly
To bring the Soul's work that The Alchemist is
attracted to
For the Soul's work is steady in the Light.

The Id Of Demand, he calls again
And he must leave my side
For the Alchemist is to take and give
The want of every Soul's journey
And when the Id Of Demand calls, he must go.

SILENT SECRET YOUR ARROW

Of increasing the pace while on the Path
Of a higher place
Happiness unlinks the path of the Soul
Traipse includes
Door unlocked
Silently shuffle inside
Then close the vault.

Then politely slide
The Keys To The Reign under the door
For the next embracer to reach
Henceforth you Silent Secret Your Arrow
When someone asks you why
You know to ask, why not?

THE SECRET WISHERS OF TIME NOT KEPT

The complexity of time
The tremors of the deep
The delicious and the suspicious
The hopeful non-malicious.
The Secret Wishers Of Time Not Kept
For they are the movers of time and space
standing not still.

Check your Time Clock Heart
Be sure you do what the Heart love flows
What deeds are here to unfold
What Hearts the love of life that can be released
To save the life of dual not told.

DANCE IN MY IMAGINATION

The minute my eyes rounded yours
I knew I would see you early
I knew we would melt into the mind.
Cold and hungry we went inside
Ate of the plate
Was neither yours nor mine
Balanced our egos
Into one weeping happy
The happy we'd see for a precious short time.
Leave us to go on
Your happy move on.

Spilled of the waiting to see you again
Heaven and Hell is in our minds.
Scattered on piles of why's goodbye
You simply had something to do.

More and more I feel each day
You wear the flesh of the skin that's mine
Moments that both will join us again
Dance In My Imagination, sick with sin.

THE SOLAR HIERARCHY

The need of mankind
Is of great need, indeed.
Hope of the world
Is on each of our shoulders
Peace in between, you know what I mean.
I wish it to stay on
Love, on the outside
Entering our Hearts from above
Crashing right through our desire bodies.

Then there is nothing that remains
But the wishes of, the Great Ones of the zenith of
The Solar Hierarchy
We must all work together
In Sacred Unison

For them is why we are here and left
And here is where I am to stay
To work my every days
A Disciple for The Solar Hierarchy
And they will take me when I'm through
And their Universe that I love.

THEE HERALDING OF TIME

Thee Heralding Of Time
Of the fashion, of the released glowing Obelisk.
The act of the force brought forth
Of the pleasing hidden unleashed secrecy.
The Cosmic Planetary Laws
Of sacred Mother Nature poureth in
Of the vestures of all past beginnings
Comes to us, in energy truth, through telepathy.

There for us to bring the knowledge within
Maybe with the sheath of my hand
Maybe with the sword of my pen
Maybe with the help of some long lost friends
Pick up on the energy, once and again.

LOLLIPOP DREAMS

The strictest rhyme
I do decline
I do endeavor today.

The simplest dream
Is what I mean
For action is beyond words.
Secret happiness, of what we seek
I think I will learn today.

Of Spirit scenes
And Lollipop Dreams
I wish you all this day.

THEE ENDLESS VORTEX

Green hills of the trees
With orange sky above, always on the rise
Glides me through the blue of water
Up into the thin of air.
Stars at moonless midnights above the horizon
Are like diamonds in our eyes.
Teleports me through time, pin point turning
Through the mist, into Thee Endless Vortex
Where your Soul lies.

And guided fantasy was the spiritual chance
And peaks we must fly to climb and glance
To see beyond to yonder roll.
Is our story to be told?
OR
Do we tell our story?

THEE GOLDEN THREAD

Touch, pinch, and then believe
Thee Golden Thread in front of me
Before my very eyes
And then woven into the fabric, of my mind
The reflection seen is brought back through
And what we seem to see
Is an optical inversion of something else.

After going through that process
It becomes part of ourselves.
Because we have fabricated
Our own impression thought
On that particular object
Making it fit
Our own stylized thought patterns.

When we look at the object
With our own personal convictions
We therefore change the purity
Of the object that we are looking at
As it was standing alone
Without our eyes.

LESSONS FROM THE FALL

The Truth is Death
Warmed over by Evil
It hurts and decays, as bad, as bad
Always leaving a scar
For its own future reference
To look back on the day
You fell on your face.

And it wasn't the fall
It was the lesson
That was learned from the fall.
And then the Truth flowed in.
And it wasn't the scar that was left on your body
It was the scar that was impregnated on your
Mind.

COSMIC SEA OF INTROSPECT

Not to be the things that I am not
I am to be the one
Of something that I've got
Something that I have
That cannot be
Is standing here in front of me
For anyone's Soul to see
You can look if you want to see.
I only thought of sweet joy
When I thought of this.
Only to let you know
That if you let me show you your Soul
I'll show you no regrets.
Caught on a Cosmic Sea Of Introspect.

THE PHILOSOPHERS STONE

Of the growth of the Cosmic thoughts
Of the greatness, of the highness, in the high
Can elevate your energy banks
Boost your lifestyle
And possibly change your Hereditary Fate
Proving that the Mind
Is the paramount ruler of all

The Alchemist having used the Mind through
Telepathy
Which was good in his lifelong span
Searching for the sign of the Sun
Reaching for the Rainbow Sky
Grasping for the Golden Horizon,
The Son was told was I.
I was told by the Sun.
The Philosophers Stone was told to me
I told myself, of the Philosophers Stone
I was told that I could not find the Stone but the
Stone would find me!
Yet we were like, we were together, and we
were.

PARADOX OF CYCLES

Life itself is a Paradox of Cycles
Interweaving our lives through the time and space of cosmic change.
Every physical and spiritual cycle intercedes itself
With the opposite face showing of it's own existence.
Night intercedes the day
And the day intercedes the night.
Therefore enlightenment intercedes periods
Of darkness of the spiritual self, does recline.

A time of cycles, of death and rebirth
A time of cycles, of joy and sorrow
A time of cycles, of peace and war
A time of cycles, of light and dark

The paradoxical cycles of life,
Lift our spirits and then let us down again
Only to continue the process of cycles
All over again
Time and space without end
Paradoxical cycles never ends.

THE RAINBOW BRIDGE

Spend some time on Purple Shores
And candy made of ice.
Bring me The Rainbow Bridge in time
And show it to me twice.
A tour in route is waiting for you
And expect it to come too soon.
I'll wait for you over The Rainbow Bridge and
meet you on Purple Shores
And will help you when you arrive.

Don't be disillusioned
Or make it difficult
It's not so really bad.
Shifting gears to Time Space Travel
Is not so really sad.

I'm going now I'm not around
I'm there, waiting for you.
I'll see you then, on Purple Shores
And hold you when you arrive.

SECRET POWER OF FIRE AND ICE

Before the beginning of time
Time itself was equally balanced through space
Space itself was equally balanced through time.
As the parallax of time and space
Intercedes, each other vortexes
The influx of time, space, and cosmic
consciousness
Creating planets and stars
With intelligence paramount survives.

Celestial consciousness of Fire and Ice
We are aware of your greatness
Both in the ethers and on high
And your physical presence here in matter
You create a paradox of fusion
Of which life beautiful itself is the spark.

The middle point between Fire and Ice
Is the middle point where life exists within itself.
Secret Power of Fire and Ice
Teach me to learn the greatness, benevolence
And the knowledge of your intelligent might.

WHEN EYEBALLS LISTEN

When you're feeling like a clown
And no one else is around
There are lots of things to see.
And though I know them well
Of all the stories I can tell
And it's all such a mystery to me.

All the many seasons that you have drawn
And the village people walk around.
And the good deeds that can be done by them
Are the blessings from within the town
And although it's not to much for me
There is really much for to see.
On the podium, When Eyeballs Listen
On the lectern, When Ears Watch.

FICKLE TOWER OF STONE

In the Fickle Tower Of Stone
Life leads on
But life leads life
And death breeds death
And hatred in the air
And love and life everywhere
Justice to live the essence as one
Living the brilliance of pure thought.
The Alchemist on the mountain is still there
Scratching his head
Wondering what to stare
If he only knew
He would come down from the mountain
He would not be barren, secret, dark and dare.

THEE FOUR ARMED CROSS

The Western Cross

The Western Cross is the way of magic
With safety from overloads
Of the power of Fire and Ice
Because each magnetic hemisphere
Is equally balanced upon both.
This is the safe upper middle path
So talked about by Mystics and Sages.

The Eastern Cross

The Eastern Cross is the parallax union
Of the four armed electromagnetic cross
And is an electrical reversal
Of energy fields
Creating an electrical field of charge
Called Fire by Friction.

The Southern Cross

The Southern Cross will make objects heavy
The Southern Cross will make things cool.
It is the direction
Where vanity stares you right in the face.
Regeneration is the spot
You're staring at right now.
Quickening time and carrying the matter
For which time was here to make
Thus becoming young.

The Northern Cross

The Northern Cross is the place to face
For the satisfied mind to rest and bathe
In the basking of the Oversoul.
Living paramount on high
Just to have being, is to feel the warmth,
Of the fires, on the face of mankind
The Oversoul is the parallax of union
Of the Four Armed Cross of the Magnetic Field
of light, time and space.

MIND BOGGLED

Stuck and mind boggled
Tough and ripped enough
Of the Garbage survivors
Of a Vulcan race.
Eating off the now dirty gray Dove
Who is nearly dead in its' mall practiced head.

Only to say that the scavengers
Live off what we pollute
Thus becoming the warhead of death.

One reason to make us all regret
Why Humanity even took its first step
Unless we knew exactly where to walk
And even then very carefully.

THE SECRET OF INTUITION

Of the reason why
Of the thought of Intuition
I can't tell you of what, why and where
But I can tell you though Telepathy
What not, why not and why
And where not to look and where to look.

The Secret Of Intuition.
We must denominate all Intuition
Then all Intuition can be used as a focal point
To learn from all Intuition
To learn of all the must nots
Thus leading a path of
Where exactly to go
We can learn the lessons of our minds
Secretly guiding us to our paths of Love and
Intuition.

THROUGH TIME AND WEAR

As same as what
As not as these
As all I want
Was what to be
Was what I was not
And that's what the Alchemist got.

He played with his life's essence
Until all the bubbles ran out.
Without swearing a word
Or promises of security
Free to the world he was.
Free to what Freedom
They would allow him to have, not much!

So much later, Through Time And Wear
The Alchemist came to be out of touch
Being very busy he didn't see anyone really very much.
He didn't give anyone a chance to criticize his secret scientific work.
He just hid in his magical world
With no one else to see the Magical Alchemy he was performing.

He started to think much clearer now.
He could even reason
Secure in the insecurity of his many hopeful dreams,
Alone!
But living his life
As one, with one Eye.

WORLD OF CHAOS AND HARMONY

In the beginning of time and space in our
Universe, after the Chaos of the Big Bang,
Stars and matter were in a state of Chaos ruling
Our Universe with dust, comets, meteors and
Stars flying aimlessly though space and time.

But though all the aimless chaos and though the
Help of gravity, time and rotation, this Chaotic
Universe though evolution in very little tiny
Solar Planetary pockets found Harmony
Paramount.
Creating Stars, Solar Systems and Terra Planet
Earth that evolved into a Harmonious Symphony
of Life.

Creating plant and animal life in which we
Evolved into intelligent human beings.
As intelligent human beings called the Human
Family on Terra Planet Earth
So today in our everyday lives filled with Chaos
In order to find Harmony in our lives
We must happily embrace the everyday Chaos
And transmute that Chaos into sweet Harmony
And this Harmony will come and shield us from
the Firefall.

THE COSMIC PARADE

My mind was altered, but it didn't falter
It shaped the spectrum, into what I desired
Happy train, see you again
All that was left was The Cosmic Parade.

Saw the spiritual direction where to go
Saw the spiritual direction where not to go
And I held my eyes in between those two cosmic places,
And it gave me the spiritual strength
To see which way I am evolving along
For you can't always predict, to your future.
All you can do is set yourself up for The Cosmic Parade.

You can set yourself up
For The Cosmic Parade
In hopes that Spiritual Evolution will happen to you
So the wonderful things that are supposed to happen in your Life, do happen.

SPIRITUALITY

Spirituality is finally in season and fashion
Of our Soul's traveling over the Cosmic Plane
Upon folding, Time and Space again and again.
Magical secrets are hidden in front of our eyes
Without any seclusion
Secrets of the hidden knowledge of the mind
Forked chasms of no regrets, of self-ambition
Torn and ripped again
By the weak, interweaving of the stitch.

TELL TALE YOUR HEART

Come on all you beautiful Lovers
Drag your Souls down the by sea.
Tell Tale Your Heart
To whomever you see
Your secrets of warmth and majesty

Then your eye catches the other eye
Of someone, who needs to be told the world
Off you go in the other directions
You broke the rules again.

But it keeps the world alive
People who love to look around.
Freedom watches the hinges on your door
A place to enter
And excuse yourself to your Soul.

SECRET LIFE

To know of your Love
In the sweetest of respects
Listen to your Heart singing
On the top of your crowning head

Of the beauty feelings, of the life not leading
Torn of the rippling sheath of Life.
The Heart is happy and strong
With much duty delight
To live, the life, of warm blood flow.

And the warmth of the Heart
And the deep feelings truly felt there
And warms and loves as long as it can
Long not disturbed, the good feelings are still
there
Secret Life, I Love you there.

YOU'RE ONLY HUMAN

The Truth is not the knowledge of itself,
But the practice, of the knowledge
Therefore knowing a Truth
And not practicing that Truth
Is not fair to yourself
Nor the people around you that you love

Misinterpreting your belief system to others
By what you say and by what you believe
Therefore, if you believe in one ideal
And practice another
You are violating yourself
Thus becoming a hypocrite
Which means that You're Only Human.

WE ARE THE KINGS AND QUEENS

Onward
Through the pages of Time and Space I write.
Poetry is of the day
And of the liking.
True Spirit, in the great adventure called Life.
The constant repetition
Of the beautiful friction called Life.
Used to the dewdrop essence
We are High People
Alive, with many worlds to Love and Conquer

We Are The Kings And Queens
That we are looking for
That we should admire and look up to
Including everyone else.

OF SPARKED HEELS OF RAIN

Of time, space and cosmic place's
To which I do mean
Upon that plain of not spoken dream's

Not matched by the Wit Of Fate
The torn reached for the hand
The un-token leaches of man
Of Sparked Heels Of Rain.

The heart, the want, the learned, the trance
The will of good
The unleashed thanks.

THEE HOUR GLASS

Thee Hourglass
The dead end street
The top of the peaks
Up against the wall
Stuck in the corner.
The wishing well
The timeless spell
The Alchemist that tripped,
Images that you cannot grip
The roulette wheel of our life
The streets of our endless dreams
We run, play and dance every night.

THE POINT OF

The Point Of, Position
The Point Of, Illumination
The Point Of, Inscription
The Point Of, Practice
The Point Of, Rotation
The Point Of, Mantra
The Point Of, No Desire
The Point Of, Humanity
The Point Of, Compassion
The Point Of, Time
The Point Of, Space
The Point Of, Gravity
The Point Of, Light
The Point Of, Spirit
The Point Of, Soul.

PAST LIFE FORMS

In richer time's not born I have seen
Shaded scenes inside my dreams.
Past Life Forms that have already been
Reach for the physical, try and come in.
Unspoken words of fate, I hear
Listen to the distance between your ears.

Un-raveled traps of life, I see.
Train gauge of life, I measure.
Dreams unlocked, of other days
Torn of what, I'm taught to see
That latter, I may live these days.

THEE AKASHIC BOOK OF THE DEAD

Find your own Akashic Book Of The Dead
It is your key to self Healing and unlocks the
Keys to your Past Life abilities
So that your Soul's future life on the physical
plane called now
Can benefit from all your creative Past Life
Knowledge from past times lived before
And incorporate your ancient creativity to enrich
Your present incarnation in your Physical form in
the now.
Thee Akashic Book Of The Dead
Is your Soul's Past Life genetic code of
knowledge.
Oh, Akashic Book that is mine
Give me the strength to have the vision to see so
deep
So that I may find my Soul's paths journey
In this present sojourning, which is called the
Paradox of Life.

THAT OF WHICH, AS IS THAT OF GOLD

You're the one who caught me
And I thank you for it every day.

You're the one who loved me
And I started to live in everyway.

The day you rushed my Soul
And green of breathing we were.

That Of Which, As Is That Of Gold
We were shining and joy was about.

That Of Which, As Is That Of Gold
Please give into me and you will see that
It's not that I don't love you
Just got a mind to live on my own.

It's not that I don't love you
I'm trying to stay at my home.

It's not that I don't love you
I'm going to keep my part for a time.

It's not that I don't love you
I need to be alone, some lonesome while.

TEACH YOURSELF TO HYPNOTIZE

The highest of nests
Of what we do fret
Is spontaneous to all of us
In the sweetest of respects

The Cosmic Forms
Relevant to our basic needs
Call on us, of all our Souls
Of all, our sojourns needs.

Shows to us of what we strive
Teach Yourself To Hypnotize
To wash the rain of the sky and sea
To glare a them, both you and me
Hypnotized together in the rainbow Sky and the
blue green Sea.

THEIR HEART'S WERE NEVER UNFOLDED

Their secrets were sold on a time line
For passage sometimes, but Their Heart's Were
Never Unfolded.
They speak of the wind
That brings them the rain
But the Magic hidden never gets learned.
We are born and die and are reborn again and
again.
Once more the Heart and Soul Reincarnates
In hopes to find, the Secrets told with in.

THE TRUTH

Breathe in the oxygen of the Truth
Suck in the power of the Truth
We are sacred spirit vessels
To drown or swim without
Our immediate attention and action
To seek the Truth without looking too far
To hide the Truth, because of easier ways of life
Objective Truth is the Truth of science.
Subjective Truth is the Truth of religion and
mythology.

Study and keep in touch with the Objective
Truth.
Conflict in a dramatic power of change
Portions of several Truth facets were invaded
Never to be seen at the scene were remained.

THE WHITE DOVE IS NOW GRAY

Lost to the world of the finite
I just can't see everywhere
Just the one bright serene place
Blinded to the dangers of Evil
It comes in many disguises
Don't know when I've been misguided
Only know that I've tried it.

The White Dove Is Now Gray.
He is hard to see these days.
You can't tell the difference anyway.
Get eaten alive
or
Eat on, to the eater.

THEE DRAGON AND THE ALCHEMIST

More than yesterday
The Alchemist tried to lead his way.
Up and going
He's always on the move.
Seen you at the scene for one second
I think I'll see you soon and again.

You've gone to waste, the Alchemist said
The apple went bad
Whose fault is that
When I see you so sad.

Don't take it out on yourself
I'll leave you alone to spy
Until you look into a brothers and sisters eye
Knowing you sold out to vulgarity
Of your mouth, mind, and body.

The Dragon tells you what to do
Through your right and left ear
Listen to the Dragon, said the Alchemist
He tells you what not to do
Then he tells you what to do
So do not listen to him.
Which conquers the Dragon as he eats his own tail.

Always have your spirit and love in motion
Move your life in the stroke of your daily Highs
Do what's best for the good of Humanity
Then Humanity will respect your motion in any
depth.

VALLEY OF THE LOST SOULS MIGHT

After the Dragon was driven away
All that was left
Anyone could say
Scourged in the tree tops
Stabbed in the alley of our life
Mixed emotions on saying it twice
Love and warmth is good advice.
Only to say you did what was right
In The Valley Of The Lost Souls Might

Gone with despair
I saw the Alchemist standing there.
Caught between where I was.
And what glowing bright vision was standing
there
I had the choice but to go between where?
Only to gaze, in glitter stare.

FERTILE FOUNDATION SOIL

Tricked and mind split
Soul, with nowhere else to go
Found, don't let it leave you drawn
Hip, what your friends appear to be doing
Ripped, doesn't seem quite so clear
Quiet, secrets are told to everyone
Longed, which no one was about to appear
Gripped, the distant voice from afar
Inapt, it was just a dream
Track, it eventually goes all insane
Loose, it sways, dangles, and drops to the ground
creating
Fertile Foundation Soil for the new kingdom
being rebuilt.

THIS SACRED SOUL TRICK

The ghost in between, you know what I mean
Love, peace, and harmony are here to warm our Hearts.
The Hearts of all our lives intertwined
Playing roulette with our Time, Space, and Gravity
Make sure to inspect them clear, so you know that it's clear.
Make sure they are all present and accounted for
Just please find your Soul's, Dharmic Path
Grasp the depth, of your Soul's wheel check
Then transmute to bliss, This Sacred Soul Trick
And have it fitted today.

THEE ALCHEMIST WAS NOT AROUND

Calling on cycles
I guess it's his time
Speaking of wisdom
I think you had won.

Dashing through the darkness
Alone with much sureness
Only looking in one direction
All he's doing is a little inspection.
Careful not to move any rocks
Careful, nice and friendly to the Magical end
Until The Alchemist slipped completely out of
town

All of sudden
Thee Alchemist Was Not Around.
No one had seen him or missed him.
He was sneaky! He laughed at the town.

www.ingramcontent.com/pod-product-compliance
Ingram Content Group UK Ltd.
Pitfield, Milton Keynes, MK11 3LW, UK
UKHW041934190726
13854UKWH00004B/1586

9 781105 471315